THE APARTMENT BOOK

A DAY IN FIVE STORIES

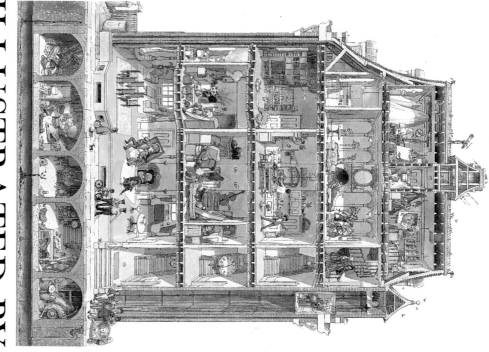

WRITTEN BY RICHARD PLATT

ILLUSTRATED BY
LEO HARTAS

DORLING KINDERSLEY
London • New York • Stuttgart

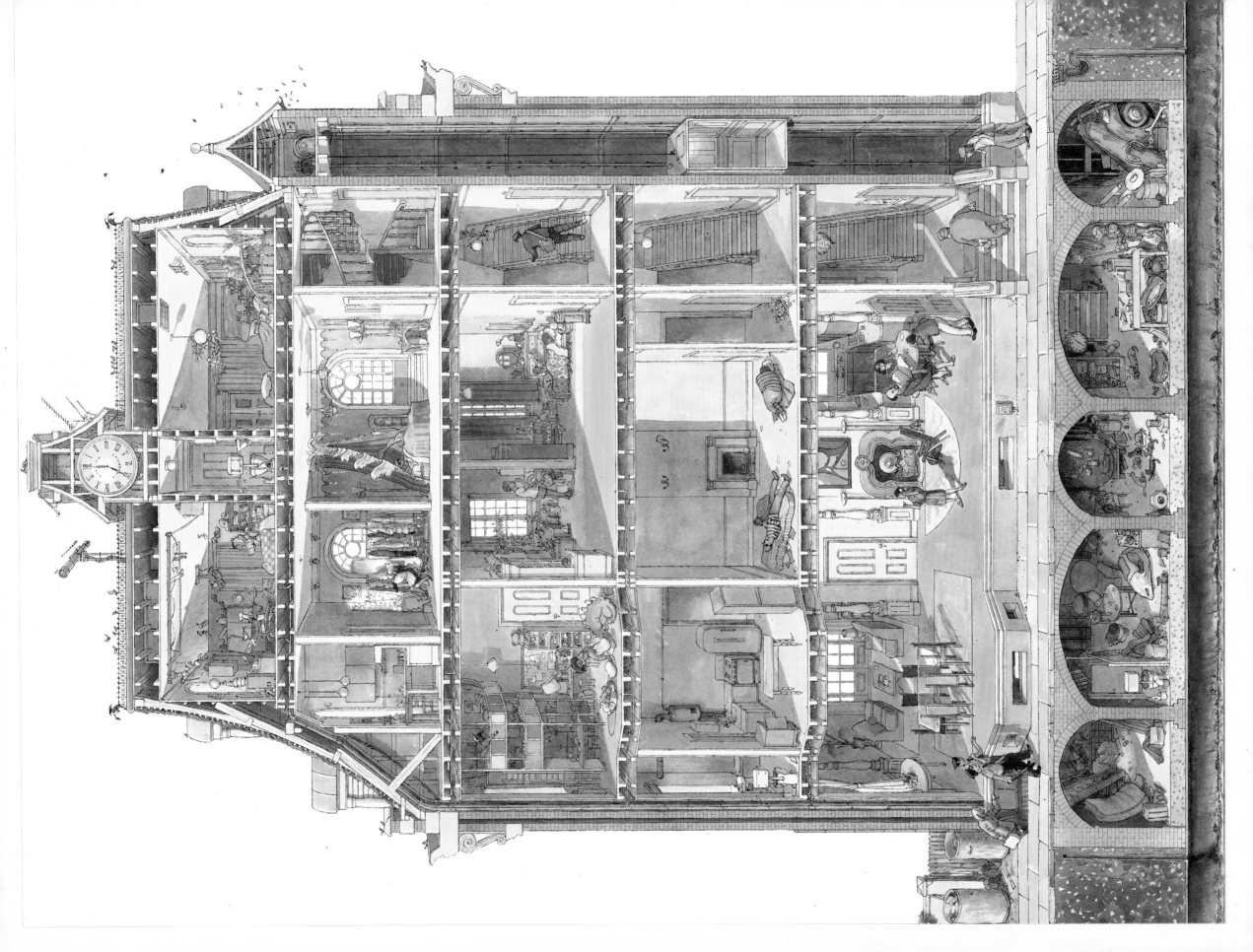

CONTENTS

For Dan

A DORLING KINDERSLEY BOOK

Project Editor Linda Martin   **Art Editor** Rebecca Johns
US Editor Camela Decaire   **Production** Catherine Semark
Deputy Editorial Director Sophie Mitchell   **Deputy Art Director** Miranda Kennedy

First American Edition, 1995
2 4 6 8 10 9 7 5 3 1

Published in the United States by
Dorling Kindersley Publishing, Inc., 95 Madison Avenue
New York, New York 10016

The apartment book / illustrated by Leo Hartas . -- 1st American ed.
          p.   cm.
Illustrates a day in the life of an apartment building by showing
activities going on in different units at various times between 7 : 00
a. m. and 1 : 00 a.m.
ISBN 0-7894-0197-5
1. Apartment houses - -Juvenile literature.   [1. Apartment houses.]
1. Hartas, Leo, ill.
HD7287 .6 .A3A6   1995
                                                        95-4662
                                                        CIP
                                                        AC

Color reproduction by Dot Gradations, Essex, UK.
Printed and bound by Mondadori, Italy

A TOUR OF THE OLD HOUSE

51 ALBERT STREET stands high on a hill overlooking the city. It began life more than 100 years ago as a family home, but has since been turned into six apartments housing 19 people. From the outside, the apartments at number 51 look tiny. But inside each one is a rambling warren of rooms. You'd miss a lot if you could only see into the front rooms, so sometimes walls have been removed to show the other rooms behind.

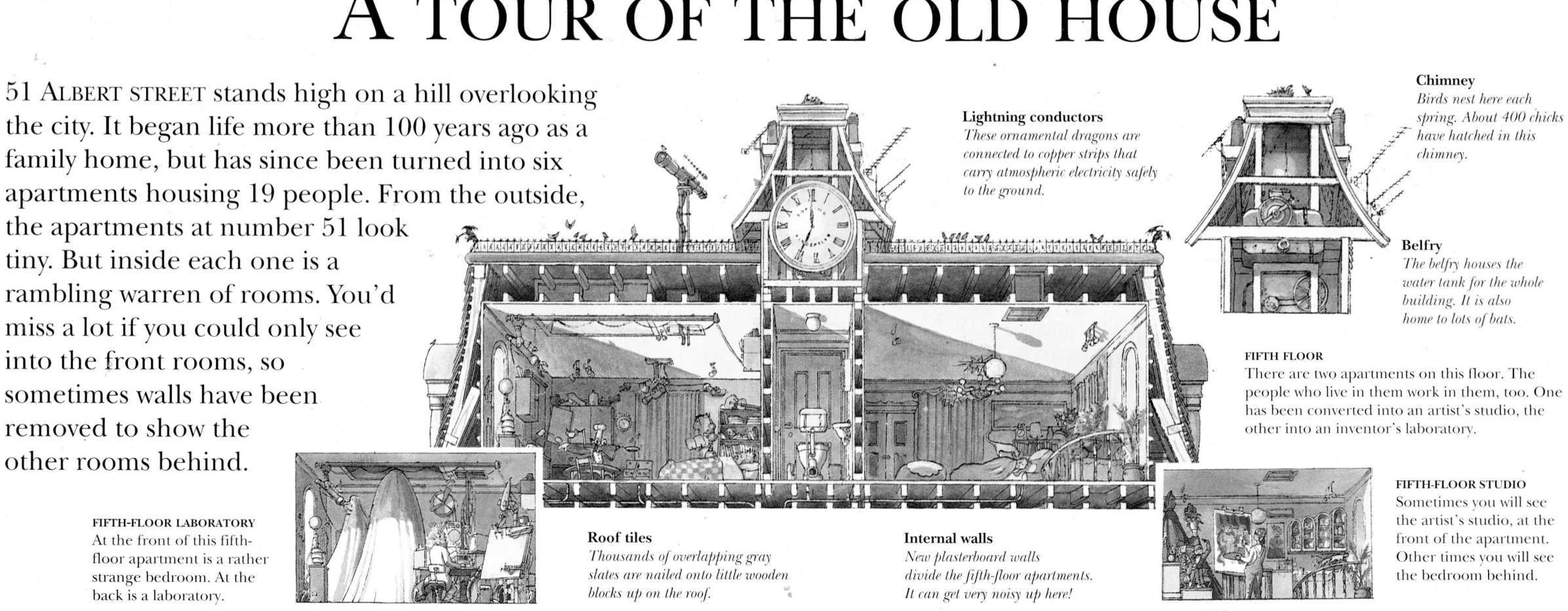

Chimney
Birds nest here each spring. About 400 chicks have hatched in this chimney.

Lightning conductors
These ornamental dragons are connected to copper strips that carry atmospheric electricity safely to the ground.

Belfry
The belfry houses the water tank for the whole building. It is also home to lots of bats.

FIFTH FLOOR
There are two apartments on this floor. The people who live in them work in them, too. One has been converted into an artist's studio, the other into an inventor's laboratory.

FIFTH-FLOOR LABORATORY
At the front of this fifth-floor apartment is a rather strange bedroom. At the back is a laboratory.

Roof tiles
Thousands of overlapping gray slates are nailed onto little wooden blocks up on the roof.

Internal walls
New plasterboard walls divide the fifth-floor apartments. It can get very noisy up here!

FIFTH-FLOOR STUDIO
Sometimes you will see the artist's studio, at the front of the apartment. Other times you will see the bedroom behind.

FOURTH FLOOR
This floor is very grand. The kitchen and splendid bedroom with connected dressing room are at the back. A famous movie star lives here.

Roof space
There are lots of interesting spaces under the steeply pitched roof. These spaces are full of pipes and joists.

Air vent
The elevator motor must be kept cool – otherwise it blows up!

Gutters
In a heavy storm, pipes drain the equivalent of a bathtub-full of water each minute.

FOURTH-FLOOR LIVING ROOM
The luxurious living room is at the front of this apartment, overlooking Albert Street.

Elevator mechanism
Housed under a pointed roof, a powerful diesel motor spins the cables that move the elevator up and down.

THIRD FLOOR
This family apartment has been divided up to provide a big bedroom for the children to play and sleep in.

The third-floor kitten loves to hide in all the nooks and crannies in the old house.

The gap between the outer and inner walls of the building provides insulation, keeping the apartment building cool in summer and warm in winter.

Each morning the pipes of the heating system creak and groan as hot water from the boiler flows through them.

SECOND FLOOR
This floor is ideal for a family. There is a living room and kitchen at the front of the house, and three small bedrooms and a bathroom (which is always occupied!) at the back.

Toilets
There are nine toilets in the house. The second and third floors and the basement have one toilet each. The other floors each have two.

Water pipes
Thirsty city dwellers need a lot of water: each day they use about 690 gallons (2,600 liters), the equivalent of 32 bathtubs-full. The main water pipes run up the inside of the cavity walls.

FIRST FLOOR
This floor has a large, open-plan family apartment with three bedrooms and two bathrooms at the back.

THIRD-FLOOR KITCHEN
Life for the family on this floor revolves around the kitchen, with its old-fashioned range. A bedroom, a bathroom, and a small living room are at the back, away from the noisy street.

ELEVATOR
This wood-paneled elevator seems to have a mind of its own; it often decides to take a day off! On these days, the fifth-floor residents have to climb 87 stairs to reach their homes.

Elevator cables
The strong steel cables that pull the elevator up and down are firmly fixed in concrete under the first floor.

SIDEWALK
Albert Street is a very busy road. Apart from the traffic, there are always lots of people walking along it. Look out for the regulars.

Basement windows
Tiny windows at street level let some light into the dank basement.

Electricity meters
This little box on the front wall houses the meters for all six apartments.

ENTRANCE
So many people have come and gone over the years that the front steps are now worn down. The front door is almost always open.

Street drain
Rainwater pours into the main sewer pipe under the house.

SEWER
Keep your eyes open for strange creatures lurking in the sewer: terrapins, escaped snakes, and even larger creatures ...

Arch supports
Strong brick arches in the basement carry the weight of the building down to the foundations.

Boiler
The maintenance men coax the boiler into life each morning, fussing around with wrenches and oil cans, curses and prayers.

Fuse box
The fuse box is in the basement. Imagine how many electric lightbulbs, sockets, and gadgets there must be in the house!

WHO'S WHO IN THE OLD HOUSE

QUITE A CROWD lives in the old house at 51 Albert Street. The grand first-floor apartment is home for the wealthy Ito family. New residents, the Ewings, are moving in on the second floor today. In the third-floor apartment above, the Normans are a fairly normal sort of family. But, by contrast, their fourth-floor neighbor is definitely not at all normal. She is quite a celebrity in fact – Stella Starspangle, the famous movie star. At the top of the house live two very different residents – an eccentric inventor and an excitable artist. And although they don't actually live there, keep your eyes open for the two maintenance men who take care of the old house.

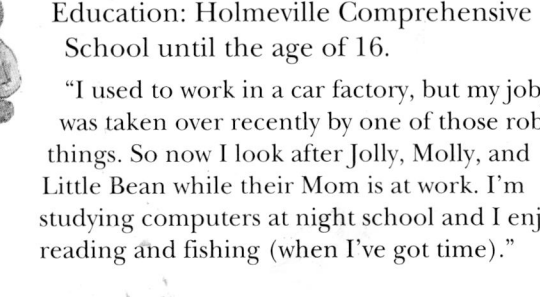

Dot Splot, the artist, spends a lot of time clearing up the mess from her paints.

FIFTH FLOOR

PROFESSOR ALGEBRUS

INVENTOR, born 1931. Physics genius, graduated from Camford University at the age of only 14.

"I used to work for NASA, but left because their Moon program wasn't adventurous enough. My ambition is to walk on the Sun. I'll land at night so that my spacecraft doesn't burn up."

DOT SPLOT

ARTIST, born 1960. Studied art at the Royal College of Painting and Decorating.

"Art is my life. I see everything through an artist's eyes: a plate of spilled spaghetti looks like an abstract painting to me. I don't have time for any other hobbies. I'm too busy sorting out the chaos that other residents cause."

FOURTH FLOOR

STELLA STARSPANGLE

STARLET, won't say when she was born. Education: Dame Shirley's Temple of Dramatic Art.

"I was discovered when I was 16 by a Hollywood talent scout. When I'm not filming (which is not often because I am always in *such* demand), I enjoy bubble baths, watching my own movies, being chauffeur-driven in my stretch limousine, and relaxing in front of a mirror at the beauty parlor."

DEIRDRE DIBBLE

MAID, born 1969. Skipped school to go to the movies.

"I'm underpaid and unappreciated: I do absolutely everything for Stella. When she's depressed, I cheer her up with chocolates. When she has a bad review, I give her advice and sympathy. I'm still her biggest fan though. I'm going to be a star myself, you know. I'm sure I'll be discovered any day now!"

THIRD FLOOR

Little Bean Norman, who hasn't learned to talk yet!

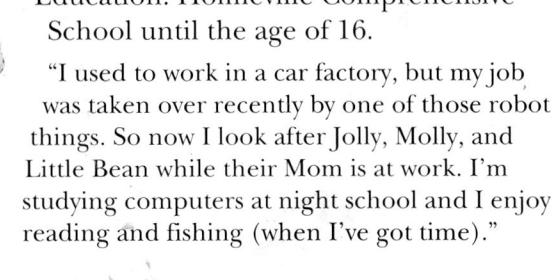

DAD NORMAN

UNEMPLOYED, born 1958. Education: Holmeville Comprehensive School until the age of 16.

"I used to work in a car factory, but my job was taken over recently by one of those robot things. So now I look after Jolly, Molly, and Little Bean while their Mom is at work. I'm studying computers at night school and I enjoy reading and fishing (when I've got time)."

MOLLY NORMAN

STUDENT, born 1984. Education: Hillside Junior School. Twin sister to Jolly.

"I'd like to be a doctor like Mom when I grow up. I enjoy school, and like swimming and reading when I'm not doing my homework."

JOLLY NORMAN

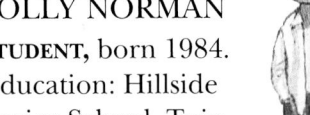

STUDENT, born 1984. Education: Hillside Junior School. Twin brother to Molly.

"My most favorite things are cooking, avoiding Hillside Junior School, softball, and playing with our pet kitten. I also belong to the Albert Street Gang."

MOM NORMAN

DOCTOR, born 1960. Education: Chopitov Medical School.

"I met Dad at a concert in 1982, and married him the following year. I'm a doctor, which means I often have to work at strange times of the day. I love reading and fishing (when I've got time)."

ELVIS EWING

BASS GUITARIST, born 1965. Education: graduated second in his class at Gracelands School.

"When I'm not playing my guitar or doing jobs for Eljay, I mess around with my motorcycle."

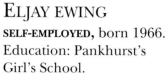

ELJAY EWING

SELF-EMPLOYED, born 1966. Education: Pankhurst's Girl's School.

"I dropped out of college to marry Elvis. I have my own pet store now, and work as a volunteer counselor at a women's shelter."

BIG TROUBLE EWING

STUDENT (on and off), born 1986. Education: Hillside Junior School.

"I hate school, quiet, and animals. I love playing tricks and generally causing as many problems as possible."

LITTLE TROUBLE EWING

STUDENT, born 1987. Education: Hillside Junior School.

"I love doing everything Big Trouble does. Mom says I'm twice as noisy and much more messy than my brother, but it's not true!"

GRANDMA EWING

DANCER (resting), born 1935. Education: Over-the-Rainbow Ballet School.

"People say that I'm forgetful, but I'm not! I can remember *all* my dance steps. I enjoy knitting and playing with my lovely grandchildren. Now, where did I put my glasses?"

GRANDPA EWING

RETIRED STEAM ENGINE DRIVER, born 1936. Education: School of Life.

"I was injured in the war and met Grandma in the hospital, where she was a nurse. I enjoy dabbling in the kitchen, but there's nothing to beat an engine furnace for cooking on."

FIRST FLOOR

OPHELIA ITO

CONNOISSEUR, born 1945. Education: the best money can buy.

"I met Oscar when he was a penniless student. Our shared interest in art drew us together, although he didn't much like my designer clothes and new-wave jewelry. I simply *love* shopping. I *have* to buy at least one thing every day."

OLIVIA ITO

FASHION SALES ASSISTANT, born 1978. Education: Finnish Finishing School.

"I don't earn much, but I like to dress well: Mommy gives me extra money for clothes. I've got four boyfriends – Nick, Rick, Mick, and Dick – and Vic is pretty nice as well!"

ORLANDO ITO

UNEMPLOYED, born 1977. Education: at home by private tutor.

"I tend to live a nocturnal existence. I emerge batlike at dusk to check out the city's trendiest clubs. When I'm not clubbing, I spend my time partying (when I wake up in time that is)."

OSCAR ITO

GALLERY ADMINISTRATOR, born 1940. Education: Tokyo Art School.

"I'm Curator of Very Odd Paintings at the City Museum of Peculiar Modern Art. I've spent the last 15 years writing a book called *Modern Art Explained*, but should finish it soon. I'm rather accident prone, which can be a disadvantage in my line of work."

BASEMENT

CARL CONDUIT

CARETAKER, born 1935. Education: Plymouth Plumbing School.

"I'm a handyman and plumber. I'll tackle any problem – don't see the need for so-called experts myself. When I'm not fixing things, I spend as much time as I can doing water sports."

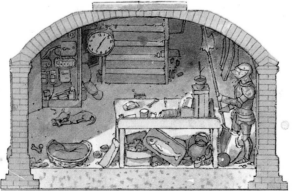

DR. JO TOOGOOD

JANITOR, born 1965. Education: City University, Sorbonne (Paris), and Harvard.

"Of course, I'm only working as a janitor to support my studies for a third degree in quantum astrophysics. I like chatting to Professor Algebrus when I've got the time. But I don't always agree with a lot of his theories! I enjoy reading philosophy, cosmology, and psychology books in my spare time."

7 O'CLOCK IN THE MORNING

THE APARTMENT BUILDING comes to life as the residents wake and get up. It's Saturday and everybody is looking forward to the weekend.

"How long have you been hanging around this neighborhood?"

"Zzzzzzzz"

"Today a great movie director is finally going to discover *me* and whisk me away to Hollywood."

"Zzzzzzzzz"

"Careful of the kitten, Molly!"

"Boring letters today. Nothing but bills from insurance companies."

"Hello, Susie! Listen, I'm having a party tonight ... NO! A VERY small one."

"I think this is the quietest building around here."

"This will be the perfect burglary. At last I'll have enough money to move out of this crummy neighborhood."

"I know you said you would be late, but this is ridiculous!"

"I wonder what's in my lunch box. I feel like a treat today."

"This looks like just the place for a short nap."

"I'm starving. What are we going to have for breakfast?"

8:30 IN THE MORNING

As a new family moves in on the second floor, the day is just beginning in some other apartments. The soundest sleepers doze on, in spite of the bangs and crashes of the moving men.

"This clock is a bit rusty. But at least it's still attached securely."

"I knew it was a mistake to paint a canary!"

"Whoa! I think I need to work on the robot's timing program. It looks like my breakfast was cooked ages ago."

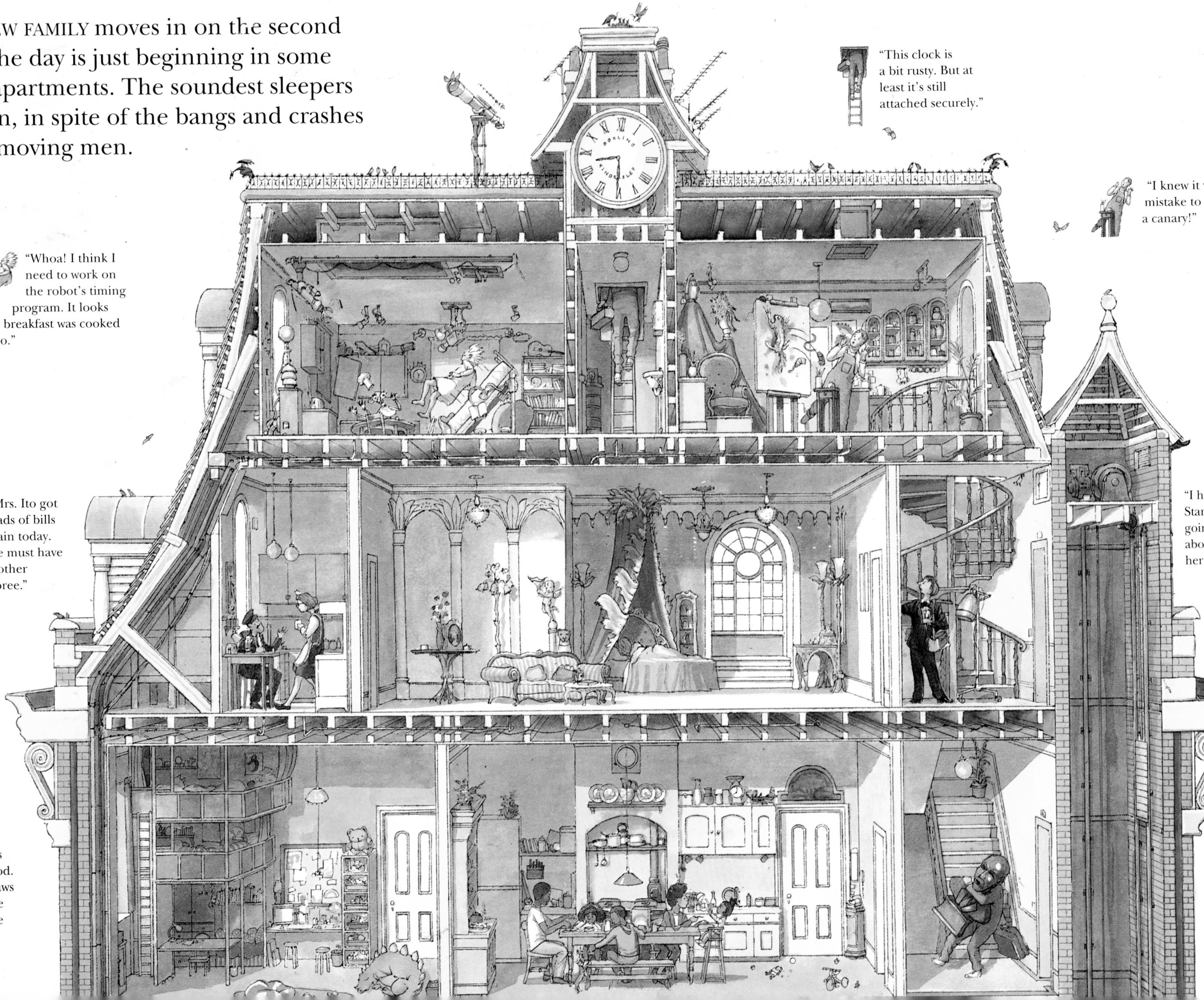

"Mrs. Ito got loads of bills again today. She must have been on another shopping spree."

"I hope Madame Starspangle isn't going to complain about me pulling her hair today."

"Our kitty is so good. He never claws the furniture or hides, like most cats."

"Where am I? Oh no! I've climbed up too many stairs – and this weighs a ton!"

"Grandpa! Your pipe is a fire hazard. You're going to cause an explosion if you smoke in here."

"I *promise*, Oscar, I'll buy only *small* sculptures at the gallery."

"I'll push, you pull. Whoa, gently does it!"

"This apartment is huge compared to our last place. How are we going to fill all this space?"

"Quick, let's hide in the elevator shaft."

 "Our first trick of the day!"

 "Delicious!" ... "No, too much black pepper, not enough tuna." ... "Compliments to the chef!" ... "Purrr-fect."

 "Do you think anyone else knows where she lives?"

10 O'CLOCK IN THE MORNING

BY MID-MORNING, the apartments are busy with activity. Things start to go wrong as the clock is about to strike ten.

"Hmm. That seems to have got most of the rust off. Whoops!"

"Yuk! Your fur is coming out in handfuls, Puss. I hope it doesn't block the pipes."

"Magnificent! All my inventions are working perfectly. Looks like today is going to run exactly on schedule."

"Madame would like hair conditioner?" (Thinks: "Mmm, even her split ends are split – and the ends of the split split ends are split, too.")

"I'm glad I don't often deliver flowers here. I could hardly fit in the elevator with this bouquet."

"He must be *under* something, Jolly. He hasn't learned to climb yet."

"Gosh, it's 10 o'clock already – time I got some sleep. Wake me up before the party starts!"

"At least the chimney doesn't need sweeping. I can't see any soot at all."

"I've met her before. Look, I've got her autograph."

"I knew those horrible kids were up to something!"

"Come on, Oscar. Let's get to the gallery quickly. I've got a feeling this is going to be our lucky day."

"Zzzzzzzz"

11:30 IN THE MORNING

THE MOVING MEN have finished their work, and everything now seems to be getting back to normal.

"The last launch didn't go as well as I'd hoped. But with new anti-matter concentrators, my rocket should rise silently through the skylight."

"Just as well Dot called me now before the plumbing problem got out of hand. Whoops!"

"You look like the kind of kids who can sit really still while I paint you."

"Stella sounds different from most of the celebrities we interview. Apparently she prefers the simple life."

"NO! Deirdre! How many times do I have to tell you? Flowers need LOTS OF WATER! Flood them, darling, or they'll wilt."

"This *has* to be my last delivery here today."

"Yes, our kitten has gone missing. The kids are really upset. Little Bean! What are you doing?"

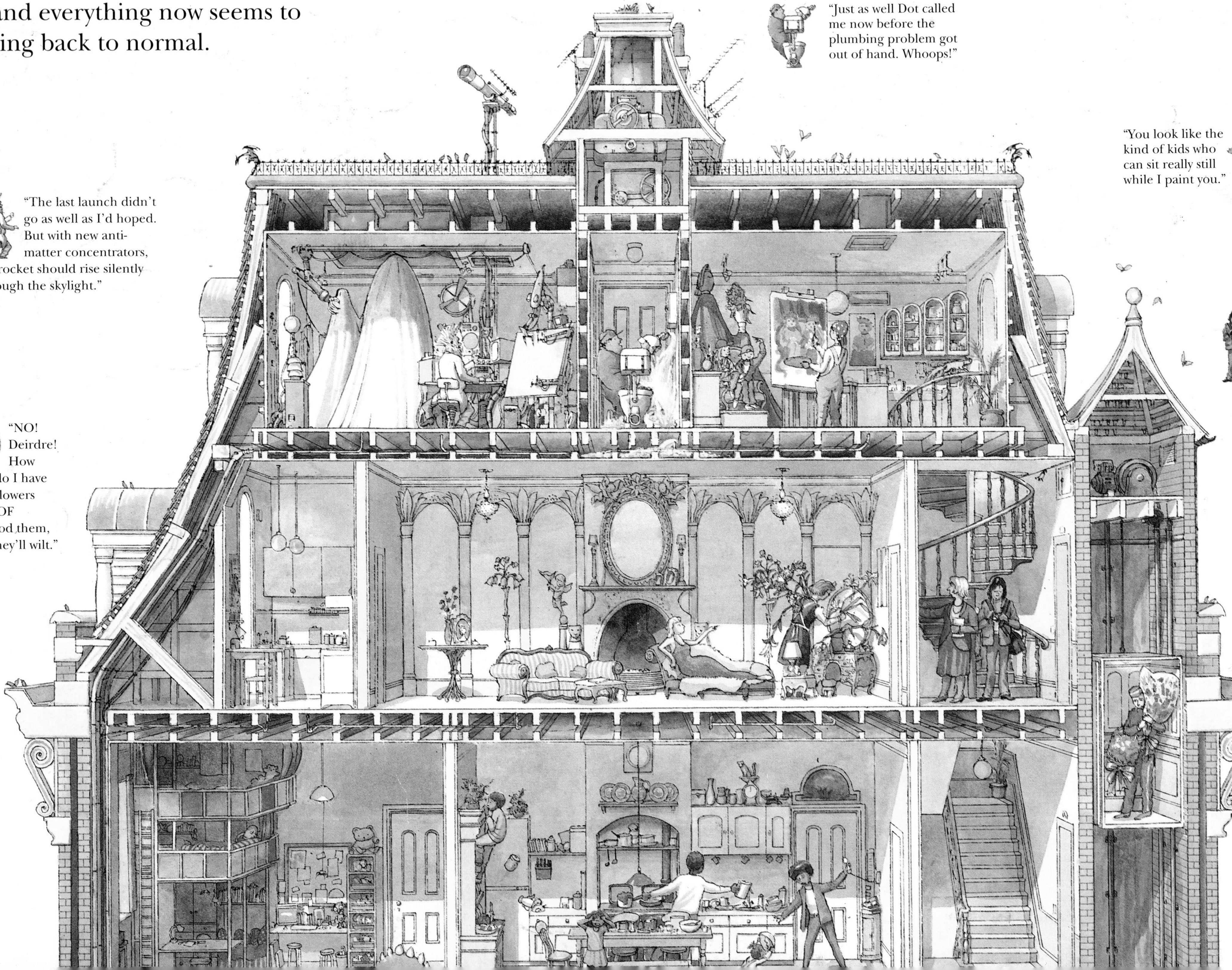

1 O'CLOCK IN THE AFTERNOON

A SUDDEN THUNDERSTORM brings rain lashing against the windows and filling the gutters. But inside, the residents are warm and dry.

"I'm not sure this space suit will be big enough."

"Maybe I'll get five minutes to myself after this."

"Whoops. I think I may need my mop and bucket soon."

"In the film I play an unlucky character, but offscreen, I seem to escape life's little disasters."

"C'mon, Jolly. The rain will have stopped by the time we get to the park."

"I'd better knit a few extra rows. Elvis has such long arms."

"Fine, bring the soloists, but we really won't have room for the choir."

"Go and find somewhere safe to smoke – like out in the street."

"Don't worry, these old houses have really strong floors."

 "Quick, the cops have seen us."

 "I wish he would leave us alone!"

3 O'CLOCK IN THE AFTERNOON

By MID-AFTERNOON, it is much drier outside, but more trouble is brewing inside . . .

"Keep calm! We'll easily clear that apartment building."

"Have you ever seen a flying cat before?"

"That's funny. The rain's stopped, but my microphone is picking up the sound of running water."

"Hmm. This sidewalk seems rather narrow."

"Maybe kitty is in Dad's hat, or on the mat."

"Perhaps he'd prefer a tie ..."

"With a small adjustment, this should really fly!"

"I can't see them anywhere, and I can usually smell a villain 10 feet away."

"Ophelia, wasn't there something on the wall above the fireplace?"

"Okay. Okay! Okay!!! They can *all* come. Are they going to wear their uniforms?"

"The interview seems to be running like clockwork upstairs. I think I'll have a cup of coffee."

"These mice look remarkably large and fierce!"

5:30 IN THE AFTERNOON

As THE FLOWER delivery boy goes up – again – Stella Starspangle's sagging ceiling comes crashing and splashing down.

"There's not been a problem yet that I haven't been able to solve."

"Phew, I fixed that just in time."

"Cut!"

"At least I won't have to put any more flowers in water!"

"Little Bean!"

"Maybe they're shooting a new surfing film in there!"

"We won!"

"Elvis! For goodness sake, stop messing around with that bike and find something useful to do."

"Now this stolen Picasso, was it a valuable painting?"

"It's good to see you children making something instead of causing mischief."

"I don't care if it is a silent order. Monks can be very noisy when they drink too much."

"It's a deal. Help me kill the rats and I promise I won't chase you ever again."

"How odd! Carl seems to have eaten all the tuna, but left the bread."

7 O'CLOCK

As the sun sets on the city, the day is far from over in the apartment building. Up on the roof, an unexpected visitor drops in.

"Fire department? My apartment's full of smoke! I think the whole house is burning down!"

"I wonder what NASA would do now?"

"Don't worry. I know this really good firm of decorators. I'll give them a call and set up an appointment."

"The only thing that idiot caretaker is good at is eating!"

"It's very peaceful out here."

"Are we having leeks for dinner, Dad?"

"Are you sure Eljay won't notice Grandma is missing?"

"Zzzzzzz"

"I know these flowers needed water, but this is ridiculous!"

"The only time those kids are quiet is when they're playing with Grandma."

"What on earth was that crash? I almost smudged my mascara!"

"????!!!!!!!!!!"

"I thought you said there were no cats or dogs around!"

DOT'S EMERGENCY CALL brings the fire department rushing to the rescue. Grandma Elvis sleeps on, and the burglars return to the scene of the crime.

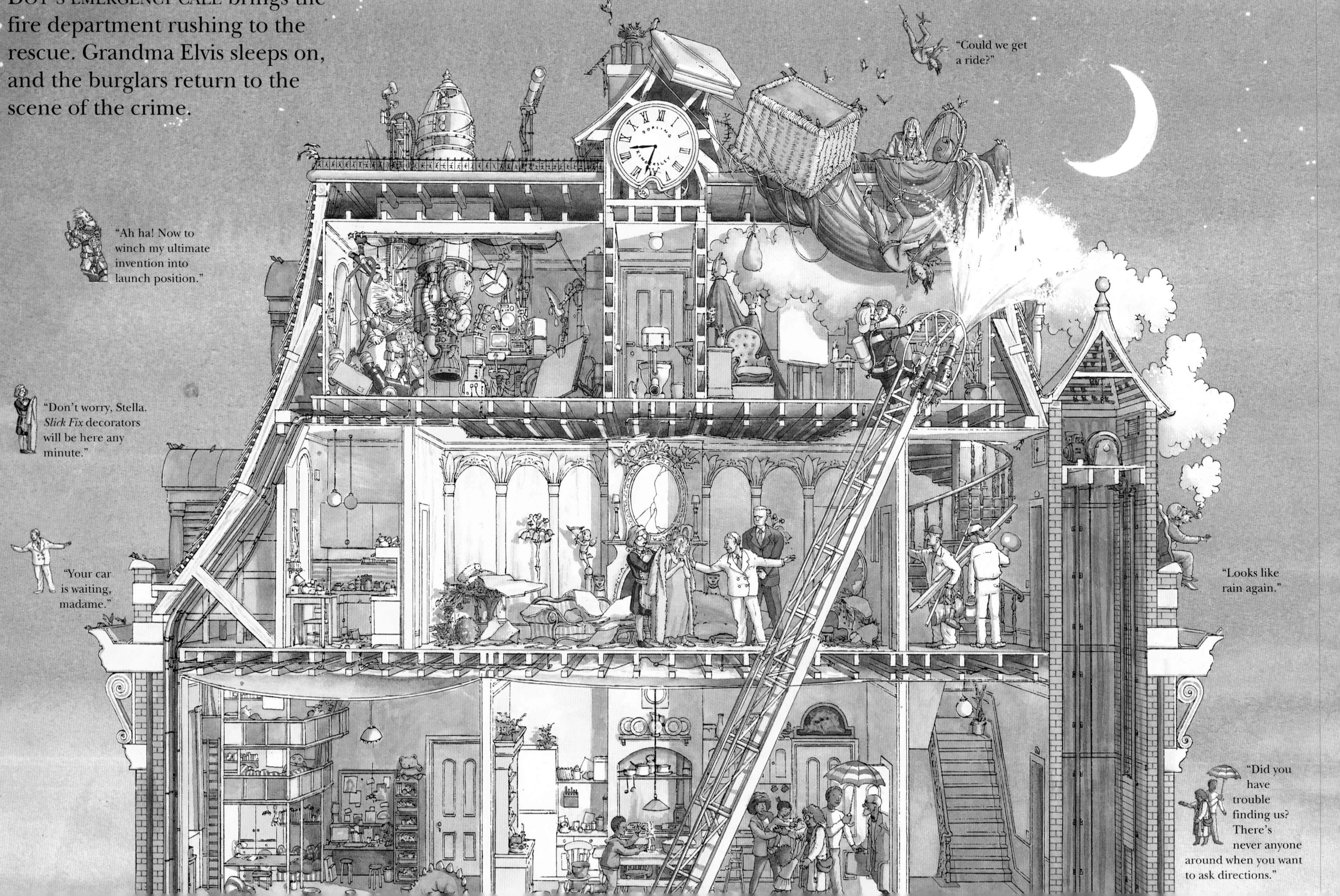

"Could we get a ride?"

"Ah ha! Now to winch my ultimate invention into launch position."

"Don't worry, Stella. *Slick Fix* decorators will be here any minute."

"Your car is waiting, madame."

"Looks like rain again."

"Did you have trouble finding us? There's never anyone around when you want to ask directions."

"Stop wagging your tail!"

"Go find Grandma!"

"OK, Mom, I promise I won't play the stereo loudly after 10 o'clock."

"Zzzzzzzz"

"Sorry, officer, I can't move the limo until Miss Starspangle is ready."

SAINT MARY'S SCHOOL
309 E. Chestnut Street
Lancaster, Ohio 43130

10 O'CLOCK AT NIGHT

THE APARTMENT BUILDING is pulsing with life. Olivia welcomes her first guests, and the Professor gets his Mars probe ready to launch.

"First stage motors igniting; powering up the gyrostabilizer."

"What a load of old junk she's got in here."

"Mmm. Looks like this pizza was worth waiting for."

"Time to clear out all this stuff."

"Oh no! All over my clean stairs."

"I wonder what Elvis is up to."

"Your parents must be really cool. Mine would never let me have a party – even a small one like this."

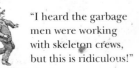 "I heard the garbage men were working with skeleton crews, but this is ridiculous!"

 "Wow! It's amazing what you can get delivered to your door around here."

 "What do you mean the limo won't move? That's it! I'm going to get you towed away!"

11:30 AT NIGHT

A MASSIVE EXPLOSION shakes the building. The lights go out, and candles and flashlights flicker in the gloom.

"Back to the drawing board!"

"Not again! How many times do I have to tell the Professor to start the gyrostabilizer BEFORE ignition!?"

"Is everything OK in here?"

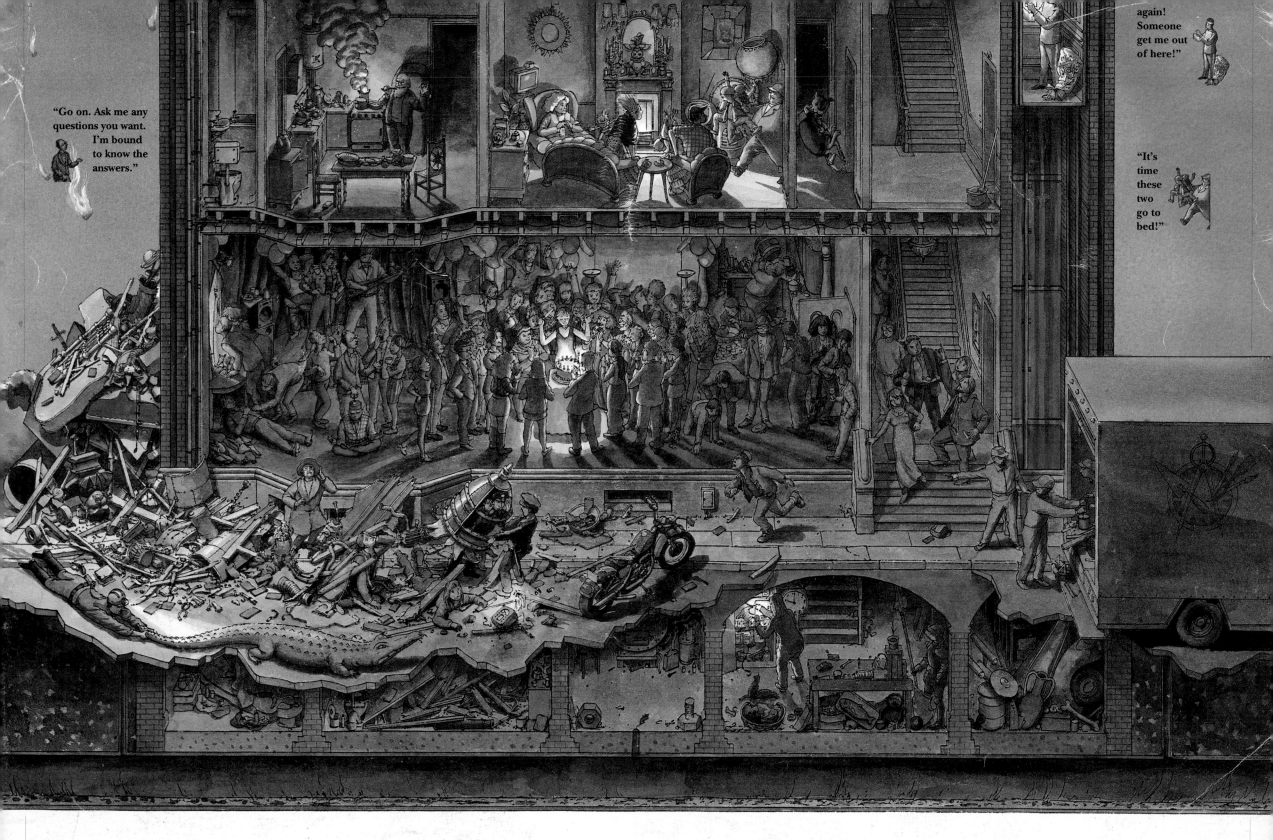

"Go on. Ask me any questions you want. I'm bound to know the answers."

again! Someone get me out of here!"

"It's time these two go to bed!"

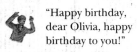
"Happy birthday, dear Olivia, happy birthday to you!"

"Let's hope it's just a fuse."

"I told you this party would go with a bang ..."

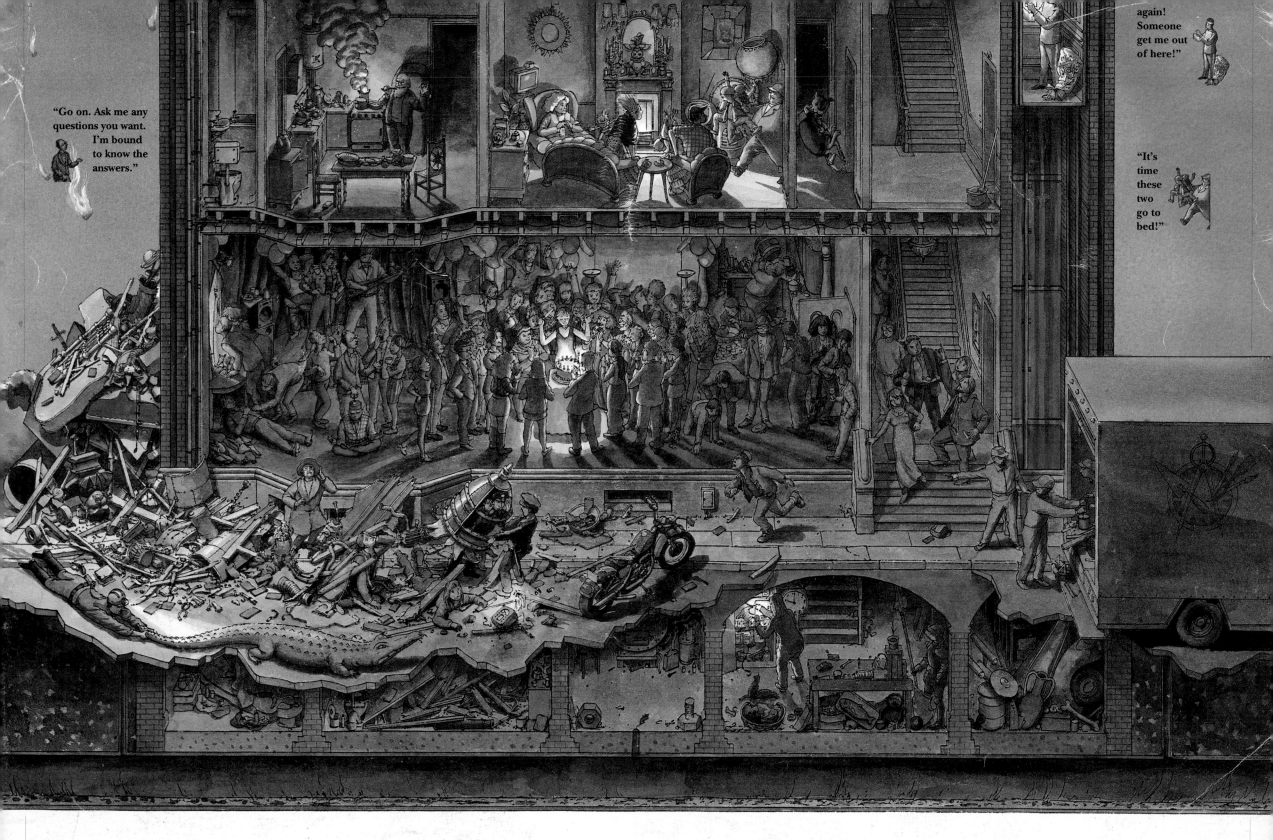

29

1 O'CLOCK IN THE MORNING

AS THE DAY ENDS, some residents
return to their beds. Others
party the night away.

"Zzzzzzzz"

"Here's to
space
exploration."

"Cheers!"

"Oh NO! What
have they done
to my
apartment?"

"Splish,
splosh,
splish,
splosh."

"Wake up,
Molly,
kitty's
come home!"

"Go to sleep,
Little Bean –
please."

"One o'clock, two o'clock, three o'clock rock."

"Zzzzzzzz"

"You smell different. Are you wearing a new perfume?"

"I love you, Olivia."

"I've always wanted to do this!"

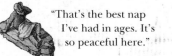 "That's the best nap I've had in ages. It's so peaceful here."

 "This beats being in bed anytime."

 "Just going to the party, officer."

 "Yeah. Well maybe tomorrow won't be so boring. Good night."

 "I'm thinking of getting another job. Nothing seems to happen around here."